CW01430116

The Truth is My L
Blessing

Presentation by *BookLeaf Publishing*

Web: www.bookleafpub.com

E-mail: info@bookleafpub.com

ISBN: 9789357442114

First edition 2023

Thank you from the bottom of my heart to my soul tribe for being that guiding light, especially whenever doubt crept in. They saw my potential before I did, encouraging me to tackle those hurdles head on. I cannot extend enough gratitude!

ACKNOWLEDGEMENT

A special thank you to the team of BookLeaf Publishing, for providing the space and opportunity to be able to put this together. This allows me to embark on a new milestone within my poetic journey.

PREFACE

My aim is to take readers on a journey which stems from my Ugandan British upbringing as well as, observations of life and society. You can find poems that come from introspective, self aware and reflective view points to uncover layers of who Grace Blessing is.

The goal is to spark a sense of healing and inspiration through the emotions behind my words and mantras!

Let Me Introduce Myself

My presence commands the room,
As my voice may speak to a few,
My energy spreads around to greet all of you.

These clothes put together to express my
creative finesse,
Some may know me for my sculptures,
Others may have felt my words spoke to them
best!
The rest may have even seen me cut a few
moves on the dance floor;
But let's lay that to rest.

My Ugandan ancestors walked in Grace,
Before me,
Heads held high with strength and glory;
And through them is where I get my Blessing,
I guess,
Thank you for welcoming me into your setting!

I know this introduction was not what you were
expecting,
I hope my spoken words take you on a journey;
Showing you a little piece of my inner being.

Grace Blessing

Note To Self

I'm far from perfect,
I know my serving may not be for everyone's
plate;
And that's okay, I come as I am.
No need to decorate or fake the real g:
Stubborn,
Difficult,
Opinionated,
Got a lot to say;
Cold,
Distant,
Too laid back depending on the day.

You see we're told to have a balanced diet,
I'm sure this is what the doctors really meant.
I'm a working progress,
That means on my time,
My terms,
The way I navigate,
Through my failures and mistakes.
Cause I gotta make sure I'm happy first;
If I'm the designated driver right?
So I may not always be so polite, especially
when:
Hungry,

Hormonal,
Tired,
If I don't get my own way;
Maybe every other day of the week.

I promise,
The rest of the time I do turn the other cheek,
Because this life isn't for the weak.
So it's okay to freak-out, sometimes,
Just a few words from the wise:
You gotta be less judging,
Give yourself more loving,
You are human;
That's just my advice!

Grace Blessing

Perspective

People ask me why I write poetry from the side
of positivity,
It's my distraction from reality,
We got a government that are okay with
breaking their own laws,
Taxing the poor,
Lack of support for communities,
Increased cost of living,
Food and other amenities.

I mean thats the real comic relief.
On top of my personal struggles,
My words are more than just a hobby or one of
my side hustles,
My light through this life puzzle.
We call society,
An outdated, unjust show of hypocrisy.
I said what I said,
Respectfully!

Grace Blessing

My Menu

Not your ordinary portion of rice and chicken,
I stand with my beliefs,
Scotch them onto your bonnet,
That's my sun in Taurus talking if I'm honest.

I like to do things my own way;
Even if it's not always right ay.
But with Pisces in my rising,
I know there's no disguising,
And moon in Virgo means my emotions love
scuba diving,
Through two colliding waves of intensity.

And just when common sense should be on time
It arrives late sipping cocktails and wine, trying
to get all the tea,
Cause yeah I'm a little nosy.
And there you have it;
Another layer to my identity.

Everyone has their own resources to help them
find prosperity or peace,
This is therapy.

Grace Blessing

Flow From Time To Time

What if the calm came after the storm?
Opening up the floor for so much more,
So that the body doesn't have to endure,
Keeping all these emotions, locked up indoors!
For you to be able to see clearly,
Let clarity have the floor,
Some may say that's a spiritual awakening,
But I feel that's your soul asking to be heard,
And that's raw!

Grace Blessing!

Fuck The Comfort Zone

When I tell you comfort,
You call me the softener,
Because I'm nice which led you to believe that
my parameters do not have a price,
You're trying to understand my area and
volume,
When I don't even know my full equation,
And you know what they say about those who
assume,
You make an ass out of me and you,
You don't even need to persuade them,
To a jury of my peers,
I the defendant is guilty for listening to my fears,
Sentenced to life imprisonment; unless I try and
do better then,
Unlearning the cycles is a long and bumpy road
ahead of them,
Me,
I mean I as in me,
I guess I need to go and find a weatherman,
To forecast the future;
Does it even get better in the end?
Look I'm not going to pretend,
I've been with you by your side consider me a
friend,

You're gonna go back and tell younger g this
story,
With all the missing vocabulary,
And then you will go and do your self inventory,
So you can grow;
But who knows what the future will behold,
I will leave you with this though,
Fuck The Comfort Zone!

Grace Blessing

Artistic Articulation

My art is my voice!
I believe it's something more than a professional choice!
It's guided by the senses I experience,
Connecting causes clarity in the mysterious,
Beauty of the curiosity.
Articulating exactly what I feel and believe;
Better yet my philosophy.
Highlighting my personal perspective of this unique crazy celestial sphere;
Empowering myself and others to embrace their true form; without living in fear.
The standards are distorted that's why they are there!
Ultimately your gift is the power to disturb,
In fact transfer,
Curve,
Shaken and not stir!
The parameters that you've outgrown,
The previous connoisseur!
After all, you only have one life to live!
So find your medium,
Allow the genuine you to premiere,
And let your voice conquer and persevere!

Grace Blessing

Soul Gardeners

Our soul blossoms because of the gardeners in
our lives;
You never know when you'll need them along
the ride.
Their light radiates throughout, our human earth
guides!

The ones who see the parts you try to hide;
The ones who push you to be your best out and
inside,
The ones who see your pride and choose to stay
cause they decided it that way,
The ones who taught me valuable lessons okay!

I'm truly grateful for everything you've done for
me,
Whether the connection is for life or just
temporary.
Energy is the purest, original currency,
That's why in life I'll never truly be lonely;

Got gardeners by my side,
homely.

Grace Blessing

Peace Intercession

Expell my words from my soul,
So that these emotions no longer take a toll,
From trying to reroll, gamble and control them,
Delayer my hill and I will comprehend,
Understanding that to heal is to attend,
For yourself facing thy true self,
To benefit my physical, mental, emotional and
spiritual health,
As well as removing the sense of overwhelm,
Excelling while repelling any negativity in and
around my realm.
Protect me from those whose put me on a shelf,
Those whose true intentions are yet to be
revealed,
Anyone that doesn't wish me or mines well!
Provide that guiding light to where empathic
compassion is upheld,
And the strength to continue being the best
version of myself!
Peace and Love!

Grace Blessing

Overthinking

Brain projecting the classics without the popcorn
and tickets,
Wonder if there'll be a time I'll ever just hear
crickets!
Front row VIP seat to 100's of thoughts a
minute,
Going round, with surround sound;
A collection of snippets,
The things that I can control all within my
limits,
It's like going thrifting in my mind;
An endless list,
Of vintage thoughts that consist of the what ifs,
On replay without a hitch,
Whilst one segment is a snitch,
The other is doing time.
While time is passing by;
Now that's the real crime!
All under the guise of 'I'm doing fine'.

Grace Blessing

Balance

Whirlwind,
Where do I begin?
Chaotic in nature;
But what about when I look beyond the danger?
It's the past, present and future competing for
space,
Yin and yang of time,
Simultaneously aligned,
Designed and defined by constructed mayhem.
Which is really misunderstood order underneath
the ticking.
Admitting that duality is at its peak,
Because sometimes your light plays hide and
seek,
Whilst waiting to be found,
While allowed to exist in the new and profound;
The darkness.
Providing a space for balance to exist!

Grace Blessing

Written By My Dream

Running around senselessly with this new found
power.
What is that? Who speaks?
The voices varied,
High pitch whispering that seemed to be getting
louder:
I'm here, see me!
Echoing from the peaks,
Where the trees, soil and flowers, spread round
and seep through;
Looked down at myself, I'm one of you!
Roots connected in;
I see myself again chasing something.
But this time I'm hovering,
Squawking: I'm here, see me!
Surely I must be dreaming,
This feels so real.
Though, tell me why I'm not screaming!?

Heaviness combined with the unsettling purple
grey sky,
There I am again, just floating by.
I don't understand what this implies.
Constantly moving with no sense of direction,
But guided by the interconnection,

I'm here, see me!
The earth was using my reflection as projection;
To comprehend its rejection,
Ignoring the language spoken;
To understand this notion of worthiness.

In the distance broke a light we missed,
A peaceful balance of yellow and golden
oranges exist,
Because yes, there is a plot twist.
The Queen Amina Nzinga insisted that I had to
learn,
Stood there firm with my soul tribe concerned.
Royalty is giving 20/20 vision to see who you
truly are,
I had failed to see that within the stars,
Which is why my settledness felt bizarre.
Because I was always moving forward,
Never stopping to admire the roses,
Or taking in the fresh air;
Of where I was.
The message is to appreciate the pause.

Grace Blessing.

Ugandan British Intertwined

Entered this Earth on my time,
Which is probably why my mum thought it
would be fine,
To take a trip to Ruhengeri, for supplies.
Well for me that was my sign to arrive!
Oops, I thought we were in Kampala City.
You know my geography is not what it's cracked
up to be.
London bound at 2 years old stayed in Chadwell
Heath.
Before moving to IG11 somewhere in between
Barking and Upney.
You know I didn't do Fish and Chips every
Friday,
Or see some of your favourite Disney films from
back a day,
I watched South African musicians such as,
Chaka Chaka on video tape,
Alongside Eastender dinner nights with the
family sitting side by side,
While eating matoke, rice with chicken stew and
g nut sauce,
Cause that's what my household prescribed!
My parents spoke to me in Rukiga most of the
time,

Which I would mentally transcribe,
translate with an English reply.
The way I grew up somethings just didn't apply,
Whilst others were naturally defined!
Ugandan by blood that I can't deny,
British by universal design.
No matter the circumstances,
I will always be intertwined!

Grace Blessing

Unrecognised Treasure

We had humanity wearing masks before the
pandemic,
Which was probably the original epidemic.
An ongoing game with poker faces so strong,
Some people believe that their armour is their
true identity.
Whilst you and I are trying to showcase our reels
on socials,
Because if the real isn't recorded on our mobiles,
Uploaded,
Gone viral,
And ready at your disposal;
Did it really happen?

Desensitised in our real lives,
Failing to realise,
That the human experience is real life,
The emotions, the trials and tribulations,
The realistic milestones we set and achieve.
The lifestyle we wish to reach without the
societal pressure,
To seek this life beyond our needs.
Comparison is a thief of joy, and a killer of
dreams,
It's easy to loose yourself in this digital regime,

But would you still compare if you had access to
every individual's behind the scene?

Grace Blessing.

The Thing About Being Introverted Is

The thing about being introverted is;
People assume that means you're:
Moody,
Shy,
Lonely,
Quiet
Or maybe even reserved.

People assume that because you're calm and
collected, that they can:
Use,
Consume,
Pick you up and drop you,
Then expect you not to utter a word.

The thing about being introverted is:
People assume that because you're not centre
stage,
You don't want to shine or grind for that same
limelight,
As though only extroverted people are entitled to
that slice of the pie!

The thing about being introverted is;
Soft spoken voices,
Often speak to personal choices.
And just because I may not be the loudest,
I may not be the most recognised.
Doesn't mean:
My worth,
My voice,
My power are not a noble prize.

The thing about being introverted is;
People insist you come out your shell,
As if this version of you is currently living in
hell!
Always looking to change, mould or assist you
into becoming this other variation.
Without even proper consideration;
Or sleep on you because they can't imagine that
version of you,
They have yet to see in person!

The thing about being introverted is;
People see you as this cry for help,
Failing,
To truly see,
The real you!

Grace Blessing.

Redefined Love

Gravitate towards the divine,
Without being afraid to shine,
Standing up for what's right.
Standing up for something so much bigger than
you.

Reliable,
Respectable,
Real.

Enjoying life through your eyes,
Is choosing to flow in today's prize,
the present.
It's choosing to show up only authentic,
in every capacity.
It's choosing integrity,
Even if that means being misunderstood you get
me.

Always consistent,
Ready to tell the truth and support me through
the blues;
Connecting with the minds,
Pushing to new heights and avenues.

Talented beyond the sense,
Understanding the universe through your mental
treasure-chest;
With a complexed combination,
You choose to bare your precious gold;
The purest soul.
That YOU entrust me to know!

And whilst there are endless words that roll off
the tongue,
There are not enough words to express my love
for you.

Grace Blessing

Future Grace

First off:
Let's start by saying thank you!
For showing me what I can do.
You know belief is one thing,
But the actions bring in the transactions I attracted.
Let's talk about the growth I enacted!
I've been a student of self;
Accumulated a lot of mental wealth,
Like how I became lovers with each version of myself that:
I discovered, uncovered, even the sides that had suffered under the covers.
Because forgiveness with gentleness is how I express my best,
No matter who or what puts me to the test.
I quote the mantra:
I'm too blessed to be stressed!

Shout out to you for pushing through your fear of public speaking,
As I know how much your internal dialogue was critiquing and freaking about taking that leap in,
Or shall I say out of your comfort zone.
I'm sure the fear hasn't completely gone,

Difference is you know you can perform,
And if you mess up, no worries; you'll move on.
The world is your centre stage,
You've performed and engaged with unique
walks of life.

You were taught, then applied what you know to
anyone who's seeking advice.
Why gate-keep?
When there's more than enough to reap.
Success, growth, strength and opportunity is best
shared then multiplied.
With loved ones, my soul tribe.
Talking about soul tribe; I can't thank them
enough for their impact and vibe,
Whether we mentally, spiritually or emotionally
connected;
To get ourselves more in check by providing and
protecting the areas we may have neglected,
It's fine to not have it all figured out yet.
Remember you're too blessed to be stressed!

Grace Blessing

Inside

You pretend it didn't happen,
Blatant lies, a regular pattern.
It's crazy cause my mind heard, what my heart
felt,
Now I'm questioning to what extent is this all
real?
Second guessing myself, playing the words said
on a cognitive wheel.
Whilst internalising the emotional ordeal.
It's hard to open up that chamber because my
brain concealed the betrayal.
The scariest thing is even though I'm still trying
to heal;
I constantly question if I ever will,
Because a part of me feels responsible for
enabling you to have power over me still.

Grace Blessing

Creator Unplugged

Writer's block feels like a disconnect from my
sauce,
I miss dripping therapeutically in the emotional
offload of course,
It's being smothered in the seasoning of
wordplay that you cannot ignore.
But my blank mind echoes like an explorator in
an empty corridor,
An overwhelming need to unlock creativity from
any cognitive door,
What had once flowed naturally,
Now feels like a chore.

Forced feeling of focus,
As if that will magically spark a light of hocus
pocus,
Shazam,
I'm still here staring at a blank piece of paper.
Hoping that if I look hard enough there'll be a
complete poem in its place later,
Becoming a stranger to something that is usually
second nature.
My creative juices float away in a manger,
Frustrations cries out as if that will somehow
wake her.

In a crib lays the dread.
The words are not flowing,
There's nothing left to be said.
Searching for my way to the pen,
So I can connect my thoughts back to my poetic
infrared.

Grace Blessing

The Truth Is My Legacy

The truth is my legacy,
I mean what's more valuable than leaving the
rawest parts of me,
The only aspect of life that's considered a
guarantee
A kinda nakedness that goes skin deep,
Its twerking to the beat of my lessons,
Making my vulnerability clap,
All while I turn the other cheek,
Caressing every curve without involving my
physique.
Because at some point the physical will decide
it's a wrap,
So I work with the sweet chilliness of time,
Instead of letting life squeeze my energy out like
a lime,
By that I mean, not just being able to savour the
beauty in the snack,
But being able to say I unapologetically didn't
look back,
Well I may have looked back at it,
But didn't go back to those negative habits.
Living pricelessly happy,
In a state of my own PH balance.

Grace Blessing

Treasure Your Worth Without Measure

Seek to be worth knowing rather than being well
known,
Since thats the beauty of letting your essence
take the throne.
Quality over quantity because it's the company
you keep that will help you flow towards your
growth,
Circle carefully radiused; makes it hard for any
thorns to edge inside your sacred home.

Seek validation from within as that way you will
always win,
The grooves,
The curves,
The scars,
And even the imperfections you may want to
change;
Is what makes your beauty truly radiate!

Finding comfort is promoted as an uncommon
lane,
But appreciate the skin that you are in;
Remember we are not all meant to look or
behave exactly the same.

If societal constructs or media platforms were
non-existent today,
Tell me;
Would divide and conquer still underplay?

Grace Blessing

9 789357 442114

The
Lemming
Chronicles

This edition first published in January 1995, with a run of 2000 copies,
by Pandoras Boox,
still an offprint of the T'Mershi Duween Group of Companies
(full details available on demand).

Prepared by Thereas Tandon
and lasar printed (wew!).

ISBN 0 9524725 0 3

Printed and generally organised
by the tremendous people
at Greenwood (Recycled) Printing,
(just for a change).

Any cock-ups, please let us know
and we'll try to correct them for a second issue
(there's nothing like optimism).